Doll Customizing for Beginners

A Complete Guide for All Materials Needed to Start Your First Project (+Prices)

By Autumn Anaxyrus (autumnsorbit)

www.facebook.com/groups/autumnsdollcustomizingorbit/

© Copyright Anaxyrus Publishing 2020 - All rights reserved.

The content contained within this book may not be reproduced, duplicated or transmitted without direct written permission from the author or the publisher.

Under no circumstances will any blame or legal responsibility be held against the publisher, or author, for any damages, reparation, or monetary loss due to the information contained within this book. Either directly or indirectly. You are responsible for your own choices, actions, and results.

Legal Notice:

This book is copyright protected. This book is only for personal use. You cannot amend, distribute, sell, use, quote or paraphrase any part, or the content within this book, without the consent of the author or publisher.

Disclaimer Notice:

Please note the information contained within this document is for educational and entertainment purposes only. All effort has been executed to present accurate, up to date, and reliable, complete information. No warranties of any kind are declared or implied. Readers acknowledge that the author is not engaging in the rendering of legal, financial, medical or professional advice. The content within this book has been derived from various sources. Please consult a licensed professional before attempting any techniques outlined in this book.

By reading this document, the reader agrees that under no circumstances is the author responsible for any losses, direct or indirect, which are incurred as a result of the use of the information contained within this document, including, but not limited to, — errors, omissions, or inaccuracies.

Table of Contents

Introduction   4

1. Essential Things to Know Before You Start   6

2. Picking the Perfect Doll   8

3. Materials to Bring the Face to Life   11

4. Everything Needed for Hair   16

5. Items for the Perfect Outfit   19

6. Artists in the Doll Community   22

Conclusion   25

Where to Buy Materials Online   27

Resources   28

For Dace and Baby Y
Thank you for always being my number one supporter in all that I do

And my mom, Lisa
For encouraging my inner artist every step of the way

Introduction

If you told me that I would be "playing" with dolls again in my twenties, I might have never believed you. Growing up, I quickly moved away from dolls thinking that they were too girly and that I needed to grow up. My younger sister continued to play with them, but there was no way someone would catch me with one in hand.

In January of 2018, Instagram turned me onto the idea of doll customizing. I had been into painting and other forms of art but seeing this was mind-blowing. Someone took a doll that was widely known across the world and turned it into something completely new. I thought to myself, "*wow, I could do so many different things*," and immediately, a thousand ideas popped into my head. I could create my favorite Tv characters, family members, or maybe even one of myself!

From then on, I was deep in the rabbit hole of the doll world. I did not want to see the light of day as I worked tirelessly on new creations in my small one-bedroom apartment. There was just too much excitement. Perhaps this is how you feel right now about the adventure that awaits you!

So, here I am today. Years into it, I've learned many things. I've had successes and failures, and for each one, I am thankful. There were times when I forgot to seal the face and wiped off the wrong part. I wasn't sure how to make **wefts** (lines of hair either glued or sewn together to make part of a wig) and even messed up the sewing on an outfit I was making. It can be challenging at times, but a finished product's satisfaction outweighs the difficult hurdles to get there. In some ways, I feel like some of my trial and errors could have gone smoother had I had something close by to help me figure out what to do.

That is why I'd like to give you what I didn't have. I just had to create this in-depth series to help you start the beautiful doll customization journey for modern dolls. I'll include real photos of my projects and illustrated ones for demonstrating how to do certain things. This first book is about all the materials you'll need to get started, including their prices. I guarantee that you'll learn so much from this guide and will be more prepared than I ever was before starting!

I cannot wait to see where your imagination takes you. I hope that you let your imagination run wild, and your hands flow with the endless possibilities in what you can create as a new doll artist. Turn this page to unleash your inner artist, and start your adventure now!

1

Essential Things to Know Before You Start

There are three things I'd like to mention before we get started. It's easy to get excited and want to start right away, but sometimes taking the time to know a few things will help you later. What I share below is what I wish I knew myself. Hopefully, you get a head start!

1. Materials: When it comes to materials, specifically ones that you use over time like glue or paints, you'll want to use an **artist-grade** (supplies that meet a specific standard of pigment load, durability, blend-ability, or some other qualities) product. It is better to use them because materials made from cheaper ingredients tend to affect the overall finished product's quality. For example, fillers in sealants can make the layers in your **faceup** (all the parts of a doll's face, including eyes, eyebrows, lips, including artistic elements such as makeup or shading) sticky over time. A sticky face means

hair and dirt cover your beautiful art long after it's finished. The number one rule is to go with quality over quantity.

2. Prices: All the prices listed in this guide are approximate (mostly based on US dollars). You may find some fantastic deals on the same products and pay only half the amount. Alternatively, you may live somewhere where it's harder to get a particular item, so the price becomes much higher. Always try to work within your budget. As time goes on, you'll be able to purchase all the things you want after saving, or even receive them as gifts from friends and family.

3. Have fun: There's nothing worse than getting excited about something to be then feeling overwhelmed. This book is simply a guide, and by no means does it mean you have to buy everything listed. Go with the absolute basics if that's your budget, or go all out if you prefer that. Either way, it's a journey of exploration and fun! You can always upgrade tools later or add more to your collection as time passes. No artist ever really starts with five-star equipment, so don't expect that you have to!

2

Picking the Perfect Doll

There are so many dolls available that you can customize these days. When you surrender to the gift of your imagination, there are endless possibilities as to what you can achieve with each doll as well. You can mix and match body parts, modify them, and so much more! Pick dolls that work best for what your vision is. Some may work better than others, but here are a few to consider when you start.

Monster High $2-10/doll: Monster High dolls are one of the most, if not the most, popular doll types among customizers. Their articulated joints and easy to work with heads make for a great project. They stopped production of these dolls in 2018 but have since rebooted two new dolls in 2020. You can find them brand new at discount stores, from people online (make sure to use caution when buying from people online), or used at thrift stores. My favorite ones to customize are Howleen Wolf, Draculaura, and Spectra Vondergeist.

<u>Barbie $2-15/doll:</u> Barbie's come in all shapes and sizes these days, making them perfect for customizing. With their new articulated joints, they are poseable! You can consider the type of skin shade and body type you want for a project when looking at Barbies. You can buy brand new, at thrift stores or people selling used ones online (make sure to use caution when purchasing from people online).

<u>MyScene $2-4/doll:</u> These dolls were a part of my childhood growing up, including the released movie. They aren't the best for posing but work just as well as other dolls of their type. They discontinued in 2011, but you can find them in thrift stores.

<u>Bratz $2-5/doll:</u> Another classic doll, and one I quite enjoy using myself. They are different body wise than most dolls, but to be honest, it's one of my favorite customs I've done to date. Today, they sell in stores under new models, but you can find the ones with original heads and body types in thrift shops.

<u>My Little Pony $2-3/doll:</u> I know, this one seems a little weird to be adding. However, MLP customs are just as popular as regular dolls! Lots of artists implement beautiful designs, like outer space, on ponies. It looks incredible and adds a unique spin to the doll community.

Ball-Jointed Dolls (BJD or ABJD) $50-1000/doll: Arguably one of the most prestigious types of beauties you can work with. They are much more customizable as each part is individually cast and strung together with an elastic string. They are considered an upgrade compared to working on the other dolls mentioned. They tend to be much more expensive than different types, and it's easy to see why. Many artists will practice on knockoffs (a copy of something that sells for less than the original product, that is not licensed and made with cheaper materials) before buying the real thing.

Honestly, I could probably list so many more dolls! There are also so many waiting to be discovered. Feel free to go online and take a look at the vast array that is available. You may find a doll that is not on this list that becomes your signature type.

3

Materials to Bring the Face to Life

I'll break this up into two parts so that it's a little easier to read. Under "Essentials" is what you'll need when creating a basic face. Everything under "Extras" are things you can use to bring it to the next level. You don't need anything from the extras to get started on your doll. Working with basic materials, in the beginning, can help you understand what you would like to have around. For example, suppose you have been designing dolls but wish you had glitter to add to the iris for every one. In that case, you'll want to consider picking up some Pearl Ex Powders before your next doll project begins.

Essentials

<u>100% Acetone $2-4:</u> Use acetone to wipe off the factory paint from a doll's face. Nail polish remover also works ($2-4). Just make sure it contains acetone. It may also

take longer to wipe off with just a nail polish remover. Remove the paint with Qtips ($2-5) or tissues ($2-4).

<u>Watercolor Pencil Crayons $20/set:</u> The pencils you use must be water-based since it reacts better with the sealant on the dolls faces. Pencil crayons will not glide onto the sealant well and will make your surface sticky when it mixes with the sealant. Some recommended brands are Faber Castell, Prismacolor, and Derwent. You can buy single pencils or sets at art stores or online. Some colors to have to get started: black, white, brown, and red.

<u>Soft Pastels $10-20/set:</u> They are like chalk. You'll want something like a palette knife (anything like a butter knife, end of a paintbrush, or toothpick can also work) to scrape off bits and make dust. You can use the dust on the face after dipping a soft, clean paintbrush into it. Using soft pastels, create shading or light coloring on the face. Use it for rosy cheeks or the look of deeper eye sockets and cheeks. Some recommended brands are Master's Touch, Munyo, Schmincke, and Rembrandt. These are available at art stores or online. I bought Munyo Pastels on Amazon, and they have worked very well so far.

<u>Pencil Sharpener $1-3:</u> Use one to keep your watercolor pencils nice and sharp! It allows for finer details when you use a point rather than a blunt end. You can find these at local supply shops, art stores, dollar stores, or online.

<u>Erasers $1-4:</u> Kneaded erasers are ones you can mold in the shape you want to get into small corners. It does a great job of lifting any soft pastels you wish to take away. Regular erasers help take off bigger mistakes. You can purchase both at art stores or online.

<u>Sealant - Mr. Hobby's Mr. Super Clear $20:</u> This is the holy grail of all sealants in the doll customizing world. You can buy a UV Flat version that doesn't turn yellow over time and will keep colors bright. Cool, dry days are best as it's quite a temperature-sensitive product. Other types you can use are Testors All-Purpose, Citadel Purity Seal, Liquitex Matte Varnish. I have not tested these brands myself, so I can not say how well they work. Lots of doll artists have claimed to have success with them.

<u>Mask for Using MSC $2:</u> You need to be in a well-ventilated area using any sealant type. Outdoors is always best, and I would be sure to wear a mask still.

<u>Cotton Gloves $5:</u> These are wonderful and make you feel professional. They keep our hand's natural oils off the doll's face, as well as keeping us clean from all the glitter and soft pastel dust. They aren't *entirely* necessary, but I think you can achieve better results with them.

Extras

Acrylic Paints $2-5/bottle: Paint is best for the most significant boost in color, detailing eye shines, etc. Not great for using as the actual face for the doll. Lines become too thick, and you lose details in the lashes.

Pearl Ex Powders $20/set: This is micro glitter. I *love* this stuff. Use it on the eyes or other parts of the face for that extra wow factor. You don't need a lot when working with this stuff. The tiny jars will last you for so long. Pearl Ex Powders are also great for other projects like resin art, paintings, and finished sculptures. I haven't tried other brands, but I'm sure any artist-grade micro-glitter will work!

Liquitex High Gloss Varnish $10: Use on eyes and lips for extra shine! Any high gloss varnish should work. Just follow the instructions on the bottle.

Doll Lashes $2: You can buy these in large quantities and cut them to your desired length. Use them on dolls to bring them to life. You can use a toothpick to apply glue and tweezers to hold lashes down in place.

Elmer's Glue-All $5: This brand of glue is much stronger than school glue. It's excellent for adhering lashes onto your doll's face. Tacky glues also work. One brand I recommend is Fast Grab Tacky Glue.

<u>Apoxie Sculpt $15:</u> Great for face and body modifications. Think horns, elf ears, protruding cheekbones, etc. The possibilities are endless. It is waterproof, air drying, you can paint it and sand it down. It's a lovely product. Just make sure to wear gloves.

<u>12g Wire $5:</u> Use wire for body mods as well. It can be the "bones" of horns on your doll or a new leg/arm (adds extra support). Sculpt around the wire.

When it comes to faceups, they are one of the most exciting parts of customizing a doll. Not only do you give them a personality, but it's something you create yourself. The possibilities are endless with what you can do. To get ideas for faces, try looking at other artists' work (without copying!) or some online photo resources. Think about how you can turn human features like eyes into more simple shapes and work with that.

4

Everything Needed for Hair

*H*air is one of the most time-consuming parts of doll customizing. You'll want to make sure that you have the proper tools on hand, at the ready, to make the process go much smoother. This list should be everything you need to get started.

Thread Scissors $4-8: These can cut off factory rooted hair on the outside of the doll's head quickly and easily. They run smaller than regular office scissors, perfect when working with little things like hair and dolls.

Long Nose/Needle Nose Pliers $8: The thinner the end of the pliers, the better. They're used to pull hair and glue out from inside the doll's head through the neck hole once you take off the head. You can also bend the wire when making body modifications.

Sewing Pins $2: to create new holes in the head or hold down a cloth to the forehead (through existing holes) to avoid getting paint etc., on hair.

Beacon Facbri-Tac Permanent Adhesive $10: This is the best glue for inside the doll head when rerooting. The glue won't melt away when you **boil wash** (pouring or dipping doll hair attached to the head into boiled water to style) the hair. Another positive to it is that it stays flexible instead of drying hard like other glues.

Rerooting Tool: You can make your own at home with a drill chuck ($10) or buy one online from a doll store ($12-15). Both will work in the same way you unscrew the top part to make room for the needle in the top. Then, you can screw it back up to tighten.

Sewing Needles $2: When rerooting, you'll need lots of these as they easily break. You can cut the eyelet with wire cutters on an angle to create the pocket required for picking up small amounts of nylon hair.

Doll Hair:

- Saran $2-5: Usually the default hair for Monster High, Ever After High, and Barbie. Available in regular, matte, color-changing, and pre-curled. You can boil wash it, but it's not the best for curling. You cannot dye it in other colors.
- Nylon $8-10/2oz: Default My Little Pony hair type. Available in regular, vibrant,

matte, glow in the dark, and pre-curled. You can boil wash, and curl easily. You can dye it with polyester fabric dye.
- Kanekalon $3-5: Resembles human hair. You can boil wash it, though it does not style well. There are very few color choices.
- Acrylic Yarn $2-10/skein: Available in a wide range of colors. You can style this very easily. Can be dyed with fabric dyes. You can find it online and at any craft store.
- Acetate $6/38": Made from deconstructed wood pulp. It has a more natural feel and is also thinner than other synthetic hair types.

5

Items for the Perfect Outfit

When you get into the mindset of creating your outfit, there is so much excitement! I always find that the more details you add, the better it can look. Think about adding trimming to the bottoms of sleeves, accessories like bows, or painting designs right onto the fabric. When you expand beyond t-shirts and shorts, the world of wild designs comes alive!

Essential

Sewing Needles $1-4: These are great when you want to sew by hand. That's how I started, and it's great when you can enhance your skills!

Thread $2-4/color: As I have mentioned at the beginning of the book, quality is something you want to focus on. Dollar store thread just doesn't do your work justice in the way that thread from an art store will. I suggest doing what you can to get a great thread. If the dollar store is your only option, double up on the line so that it's thicker and won't break as easily!

Scrap fabrics Free-$5: I love using scrap fabrics! You don't need a lot when sewing clothes for a tiny doll, so there's often an abundance around. Try using old t-shirts, jeans, or other materials that you would thrift. Sometimes thrift stores will sell scrap fabrics in bulk, or you can buy clothing materials you like and just cut those up!

Tissue paper $2: use these to create patterns for clothes that you want to make again in the future.

Extras

Sewing Machine $90-500+: While it isn't necessary to have one, it can help make the clothes making process much quicker. Sometimes outfits would take me hours, but after getting a sewing machine, I could finish certain tasks in a matter of minutes. It can really step up your game! Some brands I recommend are Singer, Brother, Babylock and Bernina. Each will have prices on the low and high ends.

Brand New Fabrics $4-20/yard: The price here will ultimately depend on the material and how much you buy. Fabric stores are lovely and have a wide array of patterns to choose from! It's always an exciting adventure going out for new outfit fabrics.

Buttons $1-4/pack: Buttons can be sold individually or in bulk. All art or fabric stores will have them. At thrift shops, they may sell them in pre-made bags with hundreds of designs. They work well for other projects, too, like eyes on a stuffed toy!

Lace $1-5/roll: You can get creative with lace. Use it as the trimming along the bottom of skirts, sleeves, or on hats. It can really pull an outfit together, and add to it in ways you didn't think possible.

Bows $1-4/pack: You can make bows for free using the ribbon you have available at home. Follow some videos on Youtube or experiment with making your own. Alternatively, you can buy small bows at craft stores in packs of 6 or more.

Flowers $1-4/pack: Flowers are the same as bows. You can make them out of ribbon at home or buy them in packs at craft stores. Try experimenting with making your own!

Jewels/Sequins $1-5/pack: The perfect addition to many artistic garments! One example is using sequins on a mermaid bra.

6
Artists in the Doll Community

*O*ver the years, many people have started sharing their journey as a doll artist online. They can be found everywhere, from Instagram to Youtube, and some even have a blog. Here are some artists I highly recommend you check out. I have learned from so many of them, including Dollightful and Mozekyto.

1. Hextian:
   https://www.youtube.com/user/HeXtian
2. Dollightful:
   https://www.youtube.com/channel/UCitKV0ebZVbtU2nIPihDGMQ
3. Mozekyto:
   https://www.youtube.com/channel/UCIc7A38DuQSZq_TZ-pi9Vag
4. Enchanterium:
   https://www.youtube.com/channel/UCXNWMCEIH99SmD52vicQ-3A

5. Etellan:
   https://www.youtube.com/channel/UCosoEuSfYCpxMhdJHp82PPw
6. Poppen Atelier:
   https://www.youtube.com/channel/UCcYRw5J5-C8plZoeZ7x2QQw
7. Oscar Magicdoll:
   https://m.youtube.com/channel/UC3ObEg3dHSn3kUAW4gY4u8w
8. Firexia:
   https://instagram.com/firexia?igshid=10k0ssft1b82b
9. Marvelousfairies:
   https://instagram.com/marvelousfairies?igshid=1k8banuyxp0v0
10. Ooakbyjuliaorel:
    https://instagram.com/ooakbyjuliaorel?igshid=z1p1I84aedq3

Use these artists to ignite your passion. Get ideas, concepts, and inspiration from them. I like to look at photos on Instagram to help me know how to draw a face. When I look at their pictures, I compare what I have to what they've done. Often, I can see details I never would have thought to include, like highlights on eyelashes or water lines in the eyes. Looking at the iris from another customizer's work can help you know how to create more depth within it. Getting inspiration isn't just about the face though, you can do this with any part of the doll. My clothing has dramatically improved from looking at work from another artist.

I'D LOVE TO HEAR FROM YOU...

If you found this book helpful in any way, I'd love to hear your thoughts in a review. Even one sentence is enough!

Conclusion

I know all too well how entering the world of doll customization can feel. It's both exciting and overwhelming. There is so much to learn and so many talented artists out there. It's hard to tell how they got to be so good and where they started their journey when you're looking at it from the outside perspective. Let me tell you, though, they all started as you did, curious.

When you have a place to start, it makes it a little less daunting. This book may have sparked some ideas or even taught you something you didn't already know, which are some of the only things I could have asked for! Maybe now you have a better idea of your first project or how to improve your current one. I know how rewarding it is getting to see your finished product after putting in so much effort!

My only hope going forward is that you continue to learn, create, and share your passions with the world. Find it in yourself to continue down the path that allows you to be who you are. When people turn their heads after hearing that you customize dolls, it can feel like a judgment. Remember that they just don't know much about it, and use that feeling to propel yourself into a creative wonderland and show them just how amazing of an artist you are.

Where to Buy Materials Online

General:
- https://www.amazon.com/
- http://www.dickblick.com/
- http://www.michaels.com/
- http://junkyspot.com/
- http://www.hiroboy.com/
- https://www.lovecrafts.com/
- https://www.lovecrafts.com/
- https://hobbii.com/
- https://factorydirectcraft.com/

Doll Hair:
- www.thefloatingisle.de
- www.dollyhair.com
- www.retro-dolls-us.myshopify.com
- https://www.restoredoll.com/
- https://thedollplanet.com/

Resources

Artist grade art supplies: Why beginners should purchase the best materials. (n.d.). Vanilla Arts Co. Retrieved December 4, 2020, from https://www.vanillaarts.com/blog/2015/4/12/lets-talk-about-qu ality-materials-artist-grade-vs-student-grade#:~:text=Artist% 20grade%20supplies%20meet%20a,or%20some%20other%20 magical%20quality

Ball-Jointed Doll Wiki. (n.d.). Fandom. Retrieved December 4, 2020, from https://bjd.fandom.com/wiki/Faceup#:~:text=A%20faceup%2 0is%20all%20of,just%20the%20doll's%20make%2Dup.&text= Because%20of%20this%2C%20many%20collectors,paint%20t heir%20dolls%20for%20them.

DOLL LAB: WHAT MATERIALS YOU NEED TO START A REPAINT? (2019, February 27). OOAK Tree Dolls. https://ooaktreedolls.wordpress.com/2019/02/27/doll-lab-wha t-materials-you-need-to-start-a-repaint/

Dollightful. (2016, July 26). *All Materials for Doll Customizing* [Video]. Youtube. https://www.youtube.com/watch?v=iBtrDdHA8y8&t=2s

Different Gotz Doll Hair Types. (n.d.). Fandom. Retrieved December 4, 2020, from https://gotz-doll.fandom.com/wiki/Different_Gotz_Doll_Hair _Types#:~:text=Wigged%20hair%20are%20%22wefts%22%2 0or,entirely%20to%20the%20doll's%20head.&text=Wigged% 20hair%20is%20durable%20and,as%20durable%20as%20root ed%20hair.

Merriam-Webster. (n.d.). Knockoff. In *Merriam-Webster.com dictionary.* Retrieved December 4, 2020, from https://www.merriam-webster.com/dictionary/knockoff

Xhanthi. (2016, November 7). *Faceup Essentials - Starter Kit Advice* [Video]. Youtube. https://www.youtube.com/watch?v=VdwSMD3Kbtk

www.ingramcontent.com/pod-product-compliance
Lightning Source LLC
Chambersburg PA
CBHW070051120526
44589CB00034B/2004